Dynamic Studies
in Philippians

Bringing God's Word to Life

Fred A. Scheeren

WestBow
P R E S S®
A DIVISION OF THOMAS NELSON
& ZONDERVAN

This book is a work of non-fiction. Unless otherwise noted, the author and the publisher make no explicit guarantees as to the accuracy of the information contained in this book and in some cases, names of people and places have been altered to protect their privacy.

WestBow Press books may be ordered through booksellers or by contacting:

WestBow Press
A Division of Thomas Nelson & Zondervan
1663 Liberty Drive
Bloomington, IN 47403
www.westbowpress.com
1 (866) 928-1240

ISBN: 978-1-9736-2289-5 (sc)
ISBN: 978-1-9736-2288-8 (e)

Library of Congress Control Number: 2018903140

Print information available on the last page.

WestBow Press rev. date: 4/18/2018

DEDICATION

I DEDICATE THIS book to my lovely wife, Sally, who is a Jewish believer. She has stood by me over the years and raised our sons in our God-loving home. The comfort of sharing our friendship and our love for Christ has encouraged me greatly in creating this series of dynamic studies of various books of the Bible. Sally's participation in our small group studies has added a much deeper dimension of richness to the discussions. Thank you for sharing your heritage, training, and knowledge.

CONTENTS

ACKNOWLEDGMENTS

MY FRIEND, BOB Mason, who at the time I began the Dynamic Bible Studies series was in his second career as the pastor of small groups at the Bible Chapel in the South Hills of Pittsburgh, suggested the overall structure of each study. Realizing our group was doing more in-depth work than most, he asked that I include several important segments in each lesson—most specifically, the warm-up and life application phases.

Bob suggested a great resource called the *New Testament Lesson Planner* from InterVarsity Press. I have augmented this with commentaries by Dr. Charles Missler from Koinonia House, the *Wiersbe Bible Commentary*, *The MacArthur Bible Handbook* by Dr. John MacArthur, the *Bible Commentaries* of J. Vernon McGee, and the whole of Scripture itself. In addition, I have also had available the *Strand Study Bible*, a gift from my friend Tom Nicastro. To make the utilization of the whole of Scripture more efficient, I have also leaned heavily on the Libronix Digital Library, perhaps the most advanced Bible software available, and other resources to help us understand how the New Testament and the Tanakh (Old Testament) fit together as one cohesive document.

I have also enjoyed the input and encouragement of my friend, Ron Jones, as I have continued to prepare these studies. Ron is a former high school principal and administrator. He is also a committed believer and daily student of God's Word. His background in education coupled with his love of God and His Word has made him a powerful force for good.

I would also like to express thanks to my good friend, Gordon Haresign, for his continued support and encouragement in my efforts to produce the Dynamic Bible Studies series. Gordon's journey began with his birth in the Belgian Congo. In the following years he was a senior executive with an international accounting firm, served in the military, labored as a Bible college professor, was instrumental in the leadership of a worldwide Bible correspondence school, and currently serves on the board of directors of Scripture Union, an international Bible-based ministry. Gordon's work as a teacher, speaker, and missionary has taken him to over 50 countries on five continents. His two most recent books, *Authentic Christianity* and *Pray for the Fire to Fall* should be required reading for all believers. Speaking of the Dynamic Bible Studies series, he has written "These are among the finest, if not the finest, inductive Bible studies available today. I strongly endorse them."

I would also like to express my appreciation to my two proof-readers. This included:

- Cynthia Nicastro, an intelligent, ardent and devoted student of the Scriptures and a meticulous grammarian.

- My wife Sally, a Jewish believer and Ivy League educated lawyer who was law review in law school, worked for the Superior Court of the State of Pennsylvania, and is now in private practice.

May God bless you, inspire you, teach you, and change your life for the better as you work through these lessons.

PREFACE

Welcome to what I hope you find to be a most enjoyable and enlightening study of Paul's New Testament letter to the believers in Philippi, which we generally refer to simply as the Book of Philippians. The letter is a very personal one and evidences Paul's great care and concern for his fellow believers in the city.

At the time Paul wrote to the believers in Philippi he was anticipating the possibility of his own torture and execution any day. Yet, in the midst of his suffering he speaks to his readers of joy and a vital life.

As we consider how this book fits into the whole of the New Testament and the Tanakh (the name used by Jews for the Old Testament, used here to emphasize the Jewishness of the Scriptures), we need to realize a number of things. We should stand in awe of this collection of 66 books, written over thousands of years by at least 40 different authors. Every detail of the text is there by design. It explains history before it happens, and comes to us from outside the dimension of time. It is, in short, the most amazing, most authenticated, and most accurate book available in the world.

If this claim is not strong enough, add to it the indisputable fact that the words contained therein have changed more lives than any others now in existence.

While the Judeo-Christian Scriptures are demonstrably perfect, my prepared studies are not. There is no way I or anyone else could possibly incorporate the depth of the text into individual sessions. I simply desire to provide a vehicle for others to use in their investigation of the Scriptures as they incorporate these timeless truths into their lives.

Speaking of small groups, Dr. Chuck Missler, a former Fortune 500 CEO, said "I experienced more growth in my personal life as a believer by participating in small group Bible studies than anything else." I believe you may find this to be true in your experience and encourage you to be an active participant in such a mutually supportive, Biblically-based group.

GROUND RULES

I DESIGNED THE first portion of each study to encourage readers to think about their personal situation. I designed the second portion to help people understand what the text says and how it relates to the whole of Scripture. And finally, each lesson ends with a discussion designed to help people apply that lesson.

You will notice that, in most instances, I have included the citation, but not the actual text of the Scripture we are considering. I did this on purpose. I believe we all learn more effectively if we have to dig out the text itself. As a byproduct of that exercise, we become more familiar with this marvelous book.

Scripture references are preceded or followed by a question or series of questions. Again, this is on purpose. I have also found that people seem to learn most effectively when employing the Socratic Method. That is, instead of telling someone what the text says and how it relates to other texts and life, they will remember it better if they answer questions about it and ferret out the information for themselves.

In a few instances, I have inserted additional commentary or partial answers to some of the questions to help the group get the most out of the study.

In addition, I added various scriptural references, intending that they be read out loud as part of the session. Shorter passages might be read by one participant, while anything over two or three verses might serve everyone better if one member reads one verse and another reads the next until the passage is completed. This keeps everyone involved. After reading these passages, I intend that how they relate to the primary Scripture at hand in Philippians be seriously considered. At times, this relationship seems to be available and obvious on the surface. In many other instances, the interconnectedness of the whole of Scripture and its principles are most effectively understood through deeper thought, discussion, and prayer.

In commenting on and discussing the various passages, questions, concepts, and principles in this material, it is not required that any particular person give his or her input. The reader of any passage may, but is not pressured to, give his or her thoughts to the group. This is a group participation exercise for the mutual benefit of all involved and many people in the group giving their insight into a certain verse or question will often enhance the learning experience.

I also have two practical suggestions if you work through this book in a small group setting. Every time you meet, I suggest you review the calendar and agree upon the next scheduled meeting as well as who will bring refreshments. This will help the group to run a lot more smoothly while enhancing everyone's enjoyment and expectations.

INTRODUCTION TO PHILIPPIANS

The Book of Philippians is one of the most beloved portions of Scripture. Here we find practical instructions from God Himself delivered through the inspired writing of one of the most intelligent and well-read human beings who ever lived. However, to get the most out of this amazing book we must first realize the background in which it was produced. The city of Philippi was of great prominence and held a very special place in the ancient world. The writer, one of the most articulate Jews to ever live, penned the letter to the Philippians from a Roman prison where he expected to receive a death sentence at any time.

Philippi was a city with a rich history and great privilege 2000 years ago. It was originally referred to as Crenides after the ancient wells and fountains to be found in the area. It was later annexed by Philip II of Macedon, one of the greatest kings of the ancient world. Philip had wanted to unify what we know as Greece and used the highly productive gold mines in the area to finance his conquests. His son, however, wanted to conquer the world.

Most educated people today are at least familiar with Philip's son. He was educated by the best minds of his time including the famous philosopher, Aristotle. He also trained under the best military experts of his time. And finally, when his father was murdered, he ascended to the leadership and conquered the known world. He was, without a doubt, the greatest strategist, general, and military leader the world has ever known. He came to be known as Alexander the Great.

What is the import of all this?

First, with the conquest of the ancient world, the Greek tongue became the lingua franca. It was and is the most precise language ever developed and has the ability to communicate meaning, nuances of meaning, and intricacies unequaled by any other. This then set the stage for the transmission of the Good News of Jesus, the Jewish Messiah, when He came upon the scene. The New Testament, which told His story in great detail and unparalleled historical accuracy, was written in Greek which enabled the great truths therein to be easily communicated to every human being with whom there was contact.

Second, this history helps to set the stage for the production of the book of Philippians. This prominent ancient city stood squarely on the Via Ignatia (The Ignatian Way), a fourteen foot wide Roman highway that connected the western world with what was then known as Asia (beginning with the area of modern-day Turkey). This was the site of an historic battle in 42 B.C. between Brutus and Cassius, who fashioned themselves the defenders of the Roman republic, and Marc Antony and Octavian, the avengers of Julius Caesar's murder. When this battle of Philippi was over, Marc Antony and Octavian (who later became Caesar Augustus) were the victors while Brutus and Cassius were dead. After this battle many veteran Roman soldiers were released from service and settled in the area.

Going forward about ten years, Octavian defeated Marc Antony in 31 B.C. Because of the assistance afforded Octavian by those in Philippi, he established the city as a military colony and conferred the "Italic right" upon the inhabitants when he ascended to the position of Emperor. This essentially gave those living in the city the same rights as if they had been living in Rome. They had, in effect and actuality, become Roman citizens.

Becoming a Roman citizen in that era and in the Roman Empire carried with it great prestige, privilege and honor. A Roman citizen had:

- Exemption from floggings and arrest (except in extreme cases).

- Exemption from the death penalty unless guilty of treason.

- Exemption from paying tribute to Caesar unlike the taxes imposed on most foreign conquered lands.

- The right to acquire, hold, and transfer land.

- The right of self-government to regulate civic affairs on a corporate basis.

- The attendant rights to vote in assemblies and stand for civil or public office.

- The right to make legal contracts.

- The right to sue and be sued in the courts and have a legal trial.

- The right to appeal directly to Caesar.

- An exclusive position as it is estimated that only 15% of the citizens of the Roman controlled world were Roman Citizens.

The apostle Paul visited Philippi on three occasions as recorded in the New Testament. He is credited with founding the Philippian group of believers when he visited with Silas, Timothy, and possibly Luke and spoke boldly of the Jewish Messiah. For greater understanding of Paul's travels to Philippi and the special place it had in his heart and ministry I suggest you first read Acts 16:5-40. Where we see recorded the details of Paul's first visit ending with his expulsion from the city as a result of the impact the new found faith was having upon the "establishment." We can also see the benefits and impact of Paul's Roman citizenship. And, we should also realize that:

1. Paul's connection with Philippi and the believers there took on a place of prominence greater than the importance of the city itself.

2. The suffering and persecution Paul endured in Philippi were much more severe than he normally experienced and seem to have been indelibly etched upon his memory.

As mentioned earlier, Paul wrote the letter to the Philippians from prison. He had been incarcerated for his faith by the Roman Emperor Nero, who in a state of mental derangement burned Rome itself and blamed it on the followers of Jesus, the Jewish Messiah. (Paul was a prisoner for four to five years. Half of this time he was incarcerated in Caesarea and half in Rome. While in prison he wrote four famous letters including the one to the Philippians, one to the Colossians, one to the Ephesians and one to Philemon. It is thought that all four letters were penned when he was in Rome. Most certainly, the letter to the Philippians was written when imprisoned in Rome as evidenced in the text of the letter itself. We see this in Philippians 1:13 where Paul makes reference to the Praetorian Guards as well as in Philippians 4:22 where he sends greetings to the believers in Philippi from all the believers in Caesar's household.) The Philippian believers had, at this point, not seen Paul but had heard rumors about the things that had happened to him and were concerned. The letter is most helpful and instructive for two particular reasons:

1. It is a very personal letter and evidences Paul's great care and concern for his fellow believers in the city.

2. Paul was daily anticipating the possibility of his own torture and execution. Yet, in the midst of his suffering he speaks to his readers of joy in the very midst of his situation and theirs.

It is my hope that we will all learn from this portion of God's Word as we study it and come to experience the joy available from a relationship with Him through Jesus Christ on an all-encompassing level.

WEEK 1

GREETINGS
PHILIPPIANS 1:1-11

Open in Prayer

Group Warm-Up Questions

In what fashion do you normally greet your friends?

In your opinion, how important is it that your greeting to a friend somehow affirms them? How exactly might this take place?

Read: Philippians 1:1-11

Reread: Philippians 1:1

With whom is Paul writing this letter?

With what term did Paul identify both himself and Timothy?

The Greek word Paul uses here for slave is *doulos*. This infers much more than the English word "slave." Read the following verses and discuss just what you think Paul meant when he referred to both Timothy and himself as *doulos*.

Exodus 21:2-6

Deuteronomy 15:12-17

In order to gain a better understanding of what is going on, let's take a few moments to understand Timothy. According to what we find in the New Testament:

1. He has the faith of his mother and grandmother. (See 2 Timothy 1:5.)

2. Timothy was taught the Scriptures from the time he was a child. (See 2 Timothy 3:15.)

3. As a result of studying the Tanakh, what the Jews call the Old Testament, he gained great wisdom.

4. The understanding he gained from his study of the Tanakh gave him the wisdom he needed to recognize Jesus as the Jewish Messiah.

5. Having understood who Jesus is, Timothy was able to make a conscious decision to trust in Him.

6. By trusting in Jesus he came to experience the salvation available through Him.

7. Paul refers to Timothy as his "true son in the faith." (See 1 Timothy 1:2.)

8. It appears to have been through Paul that Timothy's earlier preparation and study came to fruition when he personally trusted in the Messiah.

9. Timothy's decision, position, and service were apparently prophesized some time before. (See 1 Timothy 1:18.)

10. Timothy received at least two very personal letters from Paul available to us as part of the New Testament in which Paul wished grace, mercy and peace for him.

To whom did Paul address this letter?

Reread: Philippians 1:2

How did Paul greet the Philippians?

How do you greet other believers whom you have not seen or heard from in some time?

What are the two specific components of Paul's greeting to the believers in Philippi? Please list them.

1.

2.

Please note that Paul always links grace and peace together in that specific order for an observably specific reason. Please review the following verses and discuss why you think God's Word mentions these two things in this order?

1. **God's Grace.**

   • Isaiah 64:6

- Romans 3:23

- Romans 3:20

- 2 Corinthians 5:21

- Ephesians 2:8-9

- Romans 11:6

2. **God's Peace.**

- John 14:27

- John 16:33

- Philippians 4:6-7

Why is personally appropriating God's grace a prerequisite for experiencing His peace? Please explain.

Reread: Philippians 1:3

What did Paul do every time he thought about the Philippians?

Do you do this every time you think of a particular person or group of people? How so?

Reread: Philippians 1:4

What characterized Paul's prayers for the believers in Philippi?

Reread: Philippians 1:5

In what way were the believers partners with Paul?

Reread: Philippians 1:6

Of what was Paul confident? Please be sure to put this in your own words.

Why can believers today be confident of this? Read the following verses as you construct your answer.

Matthew 7:24

Psalm 125:1

Psalm 1:3

Psalm 92:12

John 10:27-28

Romans 8:38-39

Romans 8:28

Is the above referenced victory measured according to human standard or by eternal ones? Please explain.

Reread: Philippians 1:7-8

How did Paul feel about the believers in Philippi?

From these two verses, please make a list of the reasons Paul felt so good about these people.

    1.

    2.

    3.

What positive encouragement can one offer other believers?

What is the impact of this encouragement upon:

    1. Those receiving it?

2. Those giving it?

If you are privileged to be part of a group of believers, what positive things can you say about them? Please make a list.

Reread: Philippians 1:9

When Paul prayed for the Philippians, what were the specific requests he made? Please list them.

1.

2.

3.

Reread Philippians 1:10

What did Paul want the Philippians to understand?

What do you think he had in mind when he said this?

What was to be the result of the Philippians applying this understanding to their daily lives?

In practical terms, what do you take this to mean? Please explain.

To gain a greater appreciation for what is being said in this verse it is helpful to go back to the original language. First, however, let's look at the literal jump from Greek to the King James Version of the Scriptures where we read Philippians 1:10 as "That ye may approve things that are excellent; that ye may be sincere and without offence till the day of Christ."

The use of the word "sincere" is important. It emanates from the Greek word *heilikrines*, which means "sun-tested." In ancient times high quality porcelain was of great value. However, just as today, it was very fragile. It was quite difficult to put this tableware in the kiln and fire it without having it crack. When properly produced by a skilled artisan, porcelain could be held up to the sun and the surface would appear smooth, creamy and pure.

Improperly produced and defective porcelain with fine hair line cracks was not always discarded. It was often acquired by unscrupulous dealers. These shysters would fill in the small cracks with a pearly-white wax that was undetectable by the naked eye under normal lighting conditions. However, if an article of this porcelain was held up to the sunlight the wax filled cracks would appear as dark seams. Honest Latin dealers then marked their wares as "*sine cera*" which means "without wax."

How are real believers today tested and shown to be "without wax?"

How are some people today found to be like the porcelain offered by some ancient unscrupulous dealers in such wares?

Reread: Philippians 1:11

With what did Paul wish the Philippians to be filled?

The NLT puts it this way:

Philippians 1:11

May you always be filled with the fruit of your salvation—the righteous character produced in your life by Jesus Christ—for this will bring much glory and praise to God. NLT

How might you describe "the righteous character" that is referenced here and elsewhere in the Scriptures?

Read:

John 15:4

John 15:5

1 John 2:28

Romans 8:9

Colossians 1:10

Galatians 5:22-23

In what way do these references, with particular attention to the description of what is often called "the fruit of the Holy Spirit," add to our understanding of what Paul is saying in Philippians 1:11?

According to Philippians 1:11 in what way does a believer, allowing him or herself to be actively filled with the Holy Spirit, reflect upon God?

How, exactly, does this take place? Please give an example of a case of this you have seen in everyday life.

Is Paul's wish and prayer for the Philippians a good one for us to copy? Why or why not?

Application Questions

How specifically can you encourage someone in their spiritual journey this week? Please give a concrete example.

Is there a fellow believer who would be heartened to receive an encouraging note from you this week? When will you send it?

Close in Prayer

CHAINS CANNOT STOP
GOD'S OFFENSIVE
PHILIPPIANS 1:12-30

Open in Prayer

Group Warm-Up Questions

How interested are you in the lives of famous people?

How often do you read articles, books or watch television shows about celebrities?

Read: Philippians 1:12-30

Reread: Philippians 1:12

What did Paul say was the result of everything that had happened to him?

Note: The phrase translated "furtherance" in the New King James Version or different verbiage in other versions actually emanates from the Greek language and might more literally be translated as "pioneer advance." This is a Greek military term and refers to the activity of a group of army engineers and scouts that went on ahead to prepare the way for the arrival of a larger contingent of combat troops.

With this understanding of the text, what do you think Paul was saying beyond what we often see on the surface?

Reread: Philippians 1:12 in the New King James Version.

A lot has happened to Paul and it is all summarized in this one verse. For an interesting historical accounting of what happened to him after his illegal arrest in Rome, I suggest you read Acts 21:17 through Acts 28:31. Indeed, we might note that the entire book of Acts is often thought to be the legal document required to be prepared and presented prior to Paul's trial in Rome in accordance with the proceedings of jurisprudence of the time.

A short summary of these events reveals that Paul:

1. Was falsely accused by his own people.

2. Was nearly lynched by a religious mob.

3. Ended up in prison.

4. Escaped a potentially fatal flogging only by pleading his Roman citizenship.

5. Was the subject of unjust and unprovoked insults.

6. Was maliciously misrepresented.

7. Was the subject of a secret plot to murder him.

8. Remained in prison due to corrupt officials.

9. Was shipwrecked and ultimately sent to Rome as a prisoner to be put on trial.

Reread: Philippians 1:13

When Paul finally arrived in Rome after his adventures what did everyone know about him?

Note: Here we should realize that the original language says that Paul was imprisoned by the *praetorion*. This refers not to a place, but to a group of people. These people in this case were the elite Praetorian Guard who took charge of all imperial prisoners and guarded the emperor himself. This is the modern day equivalent of being in the custody of Special Forces troops such as the SEALs, Green Berets, Delta Force, and other highly trained elite fighting men.

From a human point of view some people might say that poor Paul was stuck chained to these tough warriors and what a trial it would have been. However, from God's point of view, something different was happening. Indeed, we see in Philippians 4:22 that many members of Caesar's household appear to have trusted Jesus on a personal basis as a result of their interaction with Paul.

Perhaps from God's point of view Paul was not chained to these elite warriors. They were chained to him.

What happens when we understand our circumstances as believers to be opportunities instead of trials and difficulties? Please make a list.

How can this make our words and lives even more effective in sharing the Good News of a full life through God's Son? (See John 10:10)

Reread: Philippians 1:14

How did Paul's imprisonment and conduct impact most of the other believers in Rome in general and the palace in particular?

Why do you think this was so?

Reread: Philippians 1:15-17

Why did some enemies of Paul preach about Christ with questionable motives? Please make a list.

Why did some sincere believers also preach about Christ at this time as a result of Paul's example? Please make another list.

Does this kind of thing happen today? How so?

Reread: Philippians 1:18

How did Paul feel about it when some people preached the truth for the purpose of hurting him?

How did he feel about it when people preached the truth with pure motives?

While it is obvious from the rest of Scripture and Paul's writings that he much preferred to see God's Truth preached for the right reasons, for what reason did he rejoice regardless of the motive of the speaker?

Do things like this still happen today? How so?

On what seems on the surface to be a sad note, the opponents of Paul met with some success. This especially seems so when we realize that Paul was perhaps the most intelligent, erudite and highly educated man of his time. Knowing how God used him in the transmission of His Word makes this seem like quite a crime. Upon a search of the Scriptures and other historical documents we find that:

1. Many of the so-called pastors in Rome neglected Paul and many members of their fellowships followed suit. Indeed, when Onesiphorus visited Rome and tried to contact Paul some years later he had a difficult time finding him. We see this in in 2 Timothy 1:16-17. One would think that Paul should have been respected among the Roman believers. However, he seems to have been almost forgotten.

2. The trouble fomented and results experienced by some poorly motivated speakers is evident in the writings of Suetonius, a Roman historian who said "since the Jews constantly made disturbances at the instigation of Chresus (Christ)" Claudius attempted to expel both Jews and Gentile believers from Rome. While Seutonius didn't understand what was going on with believers, he did accurately record the trouble that was created.

3. About 90 A.D. a Roman Gentile believer by the name of Clement wrote a letter to the believers in Corinth. In this letter he warned them about the dangers of jealousy among their number and the bad effect of such things which resulted in the death of many of God's people. In particular, he enumerated several examples from the Old Testament and seven from the New Testament. Among the New Testament people he cited who suffered and had been killed because of this, he included Paul. (This allegedly took place under the Roman Emperor Nero.) Jesus himself predicted that this type of thing would occur counter to His message and wishes in Matthew 24:10.

How do you think God feels about this type of thing?

How did Paul feel about it?

When I was in college I was privileged to have a professor by the name of Dr. Jacob L. Rhodes. He was chairman of the Physics department and we became friends because of my work in his classes and department. After graduating I remained in contact with him and his wife and got together with them for lunch once each summer for many years. Unbeknownst to most people was that Dr. Rhodes was one of the primary scientists responsible for the development and building of the atomic bombs used to end World War II. Many of the scientists so engaged received notoriety for their efforts, but Dr. Rhodes labored on in academia in relative obscurity. This lack of ongoing recognition, besides a few old photographs and letters, didn't seem to bother him at all. He and wife were also believers.

Why do you think Dr. Rhodes was content in his circumstances, having almost been forgotten?

How should believers today respond if in a situation similar to what Paul or Dr. Rhodes found themselves?

Why are people who have made a great contribution in their lives often forgotten by the "current generation" at many points of history?

Conversely, how should believers act toward other people or believers who have made great contributions even as these people age? Please discuss in detail. What should be the components of this interaction? Please make a list.

Reread: Philippians 1:19-20

What did Paul expect to be the result of the Philippians prayers for him?

In what way do you think Paul expected to be delivered? Was it from death or something else?

Note: At this point we might also benefit from an examination of the Biblical use of the word *ashamed*. When viewed in light of the original language, the Scriptures as a whole, and the context of word usage, it appears that a more helpful understanding and meaning of this concept is found in the word "disappointed." We can see this in the following references:

Romans 5:5

And this hope will not lead to disappointment. For we know how dearly God loves us, because He has given us the Holy Spirit to fill our hearts with His love. NLT

Romans 5:5

And hope does not disappoint us, because God has poured out His love into our hearts by the Holy Spirit, whom He has given us. NIV84

Isaiah 49:23

Kings will be your foster fathers, and their queens your nursing mothers. They will bow down before you with their faces to the ground; they will lick the dust at your feet. Then you will know that I am the LORD; those who hope in Me will not be disappointed." NIV84

Romans 1:16

I am not ashamed of the gospel, because it is the power of God for the salvation of everyone who believes: first for the Jew, then for the Gentile. NIV84

2 Timothy 1:12

That is why I am suffering here in prison. But I am not ashamed of it, for I know the One in whom I trust, and I am sure that He is able to guard what I have entrusted to Him until the day of His return. NLT

That in which we will not be disappointed (or ashamed):

1 Corinthians 15:3–4

3 I passed on to you what was most important and what had also been passed on to me. Christ died for our sins, just as the Scriptures said. 4 He was buried, and He was raised from the dead on the third day, just as the Scriptures said. NLT

At this juncture in his commentary on Philippians Dr. Charles Missler makes an interesting statement. He says:

"We tend to live in two worlds: the "sacred" and the "secular." But Jesus Christ knew no such division in His life."

What do you think about what Dr. Missler said about this dichotomy?

Please read the following verses prior to putting together your response:

John 8:20

1 Corinthians 10:31

Romans 12:1

2 Corinthians 10:5

Colossians 3:23-24

Reread: Philippians 1:21

What was Paul's main purpose in living?

For what do you feel you are truly living right now?

What do you think should be our main purpose in living?

Reread: Philippians 1:22-24

What were Paul's personal feelings about dying?

What were his personal feelings about living?

Reread: Philippians 1:24-26

Why did Paul think it would be better for him to remain alive at this point in time?

In what way would the Philippians have even more reason to take pride in Jesus Christ because of what He was doing through Paul?

In what way can we take even greater pride in Jesus because of what He is doing through certain believers in the world today? Please think of several examples.

Reread: Philippians 1:27-28

In what fashion did Paul exhort the Philippians to live?

What are the characteristics of living in this fashion? Please make a list using these two verses as your initial and primary source.

1.

2.

3.

4.

5.

6.

7.

The text makes it obvious that believers living in obedience to God's Word will have enemies. Why is this so?

Why should believers not be intimidated in any way by their enemies?

When believers depend upon the Word of God, stand firm, and refuse to be intimidated, what does this show the world at large?

Please explain how this works and give an example.

E. Stanley Jones said: "The early Christians did not say in dismay: "Look what the world has come to," but in delight, "Look what has come to the world."

How might this apply to believers today as they consider the condition of their culture, society, and the world?

In what fashion should believers respond to this situation?

Read: Matthew 16:18

Please note that this verse indicates believers empowered by God's Word, who have a relationship with Him through His Son, and are led by the Holy Spirit, are to be on the offensive and "besieging the gates of hell;" not the other way around. We are to be making a positive difference every day of our lives and in every activity.

Reread: Philippians 1:29-30

In what way herein mentioned does the privilege of trusting Jesus, the Jewish Messiah, carry with it responsibility?

Are believers to be in this struggle as lone wolves or are they to support, help, and encourage one another? How so?

At what point in life does this battle end?

Application Questions

What can you do today to encourage and help someone who is suffering because of their faith in Jesus Christ?

Philippians 2:9-11 says:

9 Therefore God exalted him to the highest place and gave him the name that is above every name, 10 that at the name of Jesus every knee should bow, in heaven and on earth and under the earth, 11 and every tongue confess that Jesus Christ is Lord, to the glory of God the Father. NIV84

What particular step can you take today toward dedicating every area of your life to the true King of the Universe?

Close in Prayer

WEEK 3

HONEST SELF-ASSESSMENT
PHILIPPIANS 2:1-11

Open in Prayer

Group Warm-Up Questions

When was the last time you had a squabble with a family member?

How much of a peacemaker are you among people who have had a disagreement?

Note: There is so much information packed into the verses we will consider today that we will utilize a number of specific lists as we study and dissect this portion of God's Word in order to attempt to get the most out of it.

Read: Philippians 2:1-11

Reread: Philippians 2:1

What qualities mentioned in this verse show that a person is experiencing unity with Jesus? Please make a list.

1.

2.

3.

4.

5.

Why is it that these qualities seem to be evident in someone when they are sincerely and diligently participating in a personal relationship with Jesus Christ?

Reread: Philippians 2:2

What are several practical ways in which believers can show their unity in Christ? Please enumerate.

1.

2.

3.

4.

Reread: Philippians 2:3-4

What thoughts and actions are we exhorted to avoid in these verses. Please list them.

    1.

    2.

    3.

Why is it important to avoid these things?

How does it affect a person if they are able to avoid these practices?

What is the impact upon an organization if people avoid acting and thinking in these ways?

How do petty squabbles hold a person back in their life as a believer?

Conversely, what qualities and mode of thought are we to exhibit as we follow Christ? Again, a short list will be helpful.

    1.

    2.

    3.

How does it impact a person's life if these qualities shine through in their interactions with other people?

How does it impact a group of believers if the members act in this fashion?

How can one honestly give assent to and thanks for their gifts and abilities while using them for good, while at the same time exhibiting Biblical humility?

Donald Grey Barnhouse said: "There is no Christian listening to my voice who will think as well of himself five years from now as he does this morning."

Do you think Barnhouse is right?

Has the thought verbalized by Barnhouse applied to you in the past? Please explain.

Do you expect the quote from D.G. Barnhouse to impact you in the years to come? How so?

Read:

Galatians 5:22-23

1 Thessalonians 5:16-22

In practical terms, what can you do to be sure you are moving in the right direction in your life as a believer? Please make a list.

1.

2.

3.

4.

5.

6.

7.

8.

9.

10.

Reread: Philippians 2:5

What overriding attitude did Paul exhort believers to have?

Reread: Philippians 2:6-8

What things did Jesus Christ, Yeshua Ha-Machschiach, the Jewish Messiah most specifically not do as evidenced in these three verses? Please make a list.

1.

2.

3.

What things can we find in these three verses that Jesus specifically did do? Please enumerate.

1.

2.

3.

4.

5.

6.

7.

What did Jesus set aside when He became a man?

How did Jesus limit Himself?

In your own words, please describe how you understand Jesus to have been fully God and fully man at the same time.

For what reason did Jesus take on the limitations of being human even though He was and is of the same nature as God?

Some people say that Jesus Christ is the ultimate example of humility and unselfishness for us. What do you think of this statement?

Read: 2 Timothy 1:7

How do you reconcile this verse with the concepts of humility and unselfishness?

Reread: Philippians 2:9

What was the result of the actions and attitude of Jesus?

Is there any place of honor above that of Jesus?

Is there any name above that of Jesus Christ?

How do you feel knowing the supremacy of the name of Jesus Christ?

Reread: Philippians 2:10-11

What will happen in the future at the mention of the name of Jesus?

It is hard to describe the highest name and position in the universe in human terms and in any language. Some of the terms applied to a high rank in the English language might include:

Celebrity.

Dignity.

Grandeur.

Greatness.

Honor.

Immortality.

Majesty.

Prestige.

Reputation.

Splendor.

Triumph.

Distinction.

Eminence.

Exaltation.

Illustriousness.

Magnificence.

Nobility.

Praise.

Renown.

Brilliance.

Preciousness.

Radiance.

Resplendence.

Richness.

While I have temporarily exhausted my vocabulary, I imagine you have not. What other terms might you give to Jesus Christ and His position in the Universe? Please make a list.

1.

2.

3.

4.

5.

6.

7.

Who, specifically, will bow their knee and declare that Jesus is Lord to the glory of God the Father?

How does this make you feel?

In what way does this impact you or should it impact you in your daily life now?

Application Questions

What practical steps can you take this week to demonstrate humility while also exhibiting power under control in your relationships?

For the sake of unity with other believers, what petty squabbles should you clear up right away? How and when will you do it?

Close in Prayer

WEEK 4

POWER FOR REAL LIFE
PHILIPPIANS 2:12-18

Open in Prayer

Group Warm-Up Questions

What is the most frequent complaint you hear?

Who pointed the way for you in your first job?

Read: Philippians 2:12-18

Reread: Philippians 2:12

What did Paul tell the Philippians to follow?

What are believers to "work out?"

In your own words, what do you think it means to "work out your salvation with fear and trembling?"

Why do you think we are to "work out" our salvation and not "work at" it?

What does this mean in practical terms?

Reread: Philippians 2:13

Is living a life that pleases God intended to be a self-help project?

How is it that believers have the ability to do what pleases God?

Note: The English word "energy" comes from a word translated "working" or "worketh" in Philippians 2:13.

What additional insight does this give you into our discussion?

To make things a little more clear, read the following verses and discuss what we learn from each reference about how the concept in Philippians 2:13 can become a reality in the life of one who has trusted Jesus.

John 14:16-17

Acts 1:8

1 Corinthians 6:19-20

Ephesians 1:18-23

People often ask, "What is this world coming to?" However, a believer might proclaim and live in such a way that an observer might say, "Look what has come to this world." How might this happen?

Read: Galatians 2:20

What further insight does this provide in terms of how a follower of Jesus today can have a life worth living?

Reread: Philippians 2:14-16

What do you tend to complain about?

What do you tend to argue about?

What are to be the component parts of a believer's life that make him or her "shine like bright lights in the world?" Please break these concepts down from these three verses and enumerate them.

1.

2.

3.

4.

5.

6.

7.

Read:

Philippians 1:27

Matthew 5:14-15

Daniel 12:3

Why is it important that believers present a positive and united front to the world at large?

How is it that the exemplary conduct of believers can encourage others to investigate a personal relationship with Jesus? How does this work?

Have you ever seen this happen in your life? How so?

How does it impact those who do not believe if those who say they follow Jesus do not exhibit exemplary conduct?

When have you seen this happen and what was the result?

Mark Twain said, "Few things are harder to put up with than the annoyance of a good example."

How does this relate or not relate to the exemplary conduct of someone who is following Jesus?

How did Paul say the Philippians' exemplary conduct would impact him?

How, in today's world, does the exemplary conduct of a group of believers impact their leaders and teachers?

Has a leader and follower of Jesus in any way been a positive factor in your growth as a believer? Who was it and what happened?

How can you have a positive impact on the growth and lives of other believers?

Read: Psalm 139:23-24

How do the concepts in these verses apply to our discussion today?

Read: Daniel 6:5

Several thousand years ago a great Jewish man named Daniel was held captive in the evil Babylonian Empire. He didn't hide. Instead he engaged the civilization, lived in the king's palace, and became his chief advisor.

In what way are we to be like Daniel?

Read: 2 Timothy 1:7

Are believers to retreat from the world and opposition or forge boldly ahead?

Note: Some scholars believe that Paul had Deuteronomy 32:4-5 on his mind when he wrote the verses we are considering in Philippians today. Please take a look at these verses and discuss how the concepts therein contained relate to our discussion in Philippians.

Warren Wiersbe says that God uses three tools, by the power of His Spirit, to work in our lives.

He says these are:

1. The unique, inspired, authoritative and infallible **Word of God**. For the effective release of the divine energy in the Scriptures he says that one must:

   - Appreciate God's Word and its power.

   - Spend time daily in the Word of God.

   - Appropriate or receive His Word.

   - Apply His Word.

2. **Prayer.** He says that to fully experience the power of the Holy Spirit one must:

   - Pray on an ongoing basis. (See 1 Thessalonians 5:17)

   - Realize and experience the close relationship between prayer and the effective indwelling of the Holy Spirit. (See Ephesians 3:20 and Romans 8:26-27.)

3. **Suffering.** While this is likely God's least popular tool it is perhaps also the most effective. For more detailed insight into this please read and discuss:

   - 1 Peter 4:12-19.

- Romans 5:3-5.

- Acts 16:19-33.

- Philippians 3:10.

In summary, one might say that this creates a snowball of growth that continually gains momentum in the life of a believer. That is that:

1. Prayer and Bible study lead to growth.

2. Growth as a believer results in having a greater impact upon the world and one's surroundings.

3. This impact will result in opposition and suffering to one extent or another.

4. Suffering drives the believer further into God's Word and prayer.

5. The process is repeated and grows in impact throughout the life of one who has trusted Jesus Christ, Yeshua Ha-Maschiach, the Jewish Messiah.

Reread: Philippians 2:17

Note: The word used for "offered" or "offering" in this verse is *spendo* in the Greek. At the time, a drink offering would be poured out as part of a pagan offering following the sacrifice and burnt offering of an animal. The person making the offering would put out a cup of wine on the still hot altar and it would disappear in a burst of steam.

Paul was in prison. Any day he knew that he might be executed. How does he say he would feel if he were to lose his life?

In what way does he say his life would be like an offering to God? Please explain what you think this means.

How does Paul characterize the faithful service of believers?

What do you think he means by faithful service?

In what way is the faithful service an offering to God? Please explain.

What is the result of faithful service to God?

Why does Paul want the Philippian believers to experience this result?

Why do you think things work this way in human experience?

Reread: Philippians 2:18

What does Paul again tell the Philippians that they should do?

Why do you think he reiterates this point?

How will it impact Paul if the Philippian believers are following God's Word and plan for their lives?

How does it impact a good teacher today if they see those they have had a part in teaching living obedient, fruitful and joyful lives?

Why is this?

Application Questions

In Ephesians 2:10 we come to understand that God has a unique plan for every one of the lives of those who have found new life in Him through His Son.

Ephesians 2:10

"For we are God's masterpiece. He has created us anew in Christ Jesus, so we can do the good things He planned for us long ago."

So far as you understand it, what is God's distinct plan for your life?

Specifically before whom do you want to "shine" as a believer at work or in your neighborhood this week? How can you do so?

In what situations do you need to not complain and argue?

What sacrifices can you make for the sake of others this week?

Close in Prayer

TIMOTHY AND EPAPHRODITUS
PHILIPPIANS 2:19-30

Open in Prayer

Group Warm-Up Questions

When was the last time you gave a character reference for a friend?

If close friends were to talk about you when you were not in their presence, what do you think they would say?

Read: Philippians 2:19-30

Reread: Philippians 2:19

Why did Paul hope to send Timothy to visit the Philippians?

What specific things did Paul expect to result from Timothy's hoped-for trip?

Why do you think receiving news of the Philippians would have such an impact upon Paul?

Under what prerequisite condition did Paul hope to send Timothy to see the Philippians?

What do we learn from this prerequisite condition and how should we apply it to our lives?

Reread: Philippians 2:20

What was Paul's opinion of Timothy?

What was Timothy's relationship with the believers in Philippi?

Reread: Philippians 2:21

With what indictment did Paul describe "the others?"

Who were these people?

Are there people today who might also fit the description of "the others" in Rome? How so?

How can we be sure to not be part of such a group?

Reread: Philippians 2:22

What had Timothy done with success? Please make a list.

1.

2.

3.

4.

What can we do to be like Timothy in the world today?

Note: Timothy's qualities and actions were obviously unusual in the society of his day. This seems to have periodically been a problem at various points of history.

Indeed, in 500 B.C. Socrates said,

"Our youth now love luxury. They have bad manners, contempt for authority, disrespect for older people. Children nowadays are tyrants. They no longer rise when their elders enter the room. They contradict their parents, chatter before company, gobble their food, and tyrannize their teachers."

How does this relate or not relate to the society in which you find yourself living today?

Reread: Philippians 2:23

When did Paul want to send Timothy back to the Philippians?

What was Paul expecting to happen to him?

If Paul was sentenced to death, what did he plan to do in relationship to Timothy, who had been such a comfort to him? What do you make of this?

Reread: Philippians 2:24

Why was Paul feeling confident that he would visit his believing friends in Philippi again?

Reread: Philippians 2:25

Also read: Philippians 4:18

What three qualities characterized the life of Epaphroditus? Please make a list.

1.

2.

3.

How had Epaphroditus served both his fellow believers in Philippi as well as Paul?

Note 1: Paul identified this man as a "true brother."

At the time he wrote this letter, the concept of someone being a believing "brother" or "sister" transcending all normal human categorizations was revolutionary. Society was divided into groups and each group was in many ways polarized from the others. Some of the groups at the time included:

1. Guilds.

2. Soldiers.

3. Jews.

4. Gentiles.

5. Aristocrats.

6. Plebians.

How does this relate to our culture in general and specifically to believers today?

Note 2: Paul also identifies Epaphroditus as a "co-worker" or "fellow laborer."

Do believers in our culture view each other in this fashion or are they sometimes so involved with the popular culture that they forget their real identity as followers of the Jewish Messiah? Please think of an example of each.

Do you feel that believers in our society are doing enough to shape the culture in ways pleasing to God on the following levels? (Please explain your answer in each case.)

1. Intellectual development including clarity and honesty of thought.

2. Social interaction including helping people with real human needs.

3. Helping other people come to know God in a personal way through Jesus Christ.

Note 3: Paul referred to Epaphroditus as a "fellow soldier."

We must remember the imagery of the day when this was written. Romans developed shoulder-to-shoulder fighting from the Greek Phalanx. The Roman shoulder-to-shoulder Phalanx was an almost impenetrable wall of shields and was a terror to many enemy combatants.

How might this have related to what Paul was talking about when he called his friend a "fellow soldier?"

What should this have to do with us today?

Reread: Philippians 2:26

How did Epaphroditus feel about his fellow believers in Philippi?

Note: This was not a short trip. Philippi was about 800 miles from Rome and traveling that distance in Paul's day would have taken at least six weeks.

Reread: Philippians 2:26-27

What happened to Epaphroditus when he was away from home and helping Paul?

How sick had Epaphroditus become when on his trip?

Is there any evidence that this man's sickness was a result of his sin, lack of faith or some offense against God?

Why is it destructive and unbiblical when one thinks of sickness in such a fashion?

Read: Romans 8:28

Can and does God use sickness as well as health in the lives of those who love and follow Him? How so?

How did Paul feel about Epaphroditus?

How would he have felt if Epaphroditus had died, even though he knew his friend was a believer and would be with God if he did succumb to his illness?

Why would Paul have been so sorrowful if he knew that his friend's eternal destiny was assured?

How do people react to the death of a loved one today, even if the one who has died was solid in their relationship to Jesus Christ? Why might this be true?

Reread: Philippians 2:28

Also read: Romans 12:3

How did Paul demonstrate his selflessness and concern for his fellow believers?

Why do you think Paul would not be so concerned about his friends in Philippi when Epaphroditus returned to them?

How did Paul say the Philippians welcoming back Epaphroditus would impact him?

Why do you think Paul expected to be affected in this manner?

How might something similar occur in our lives? Please explain.

How and why does this principal seem to operate in human interaction?

Read:

1 Corinthians 13:3-4

Luke 18:14

1 Peter 5:6-7

How should we exhibit qualities similar to what we see in Paul in the circumstance in which he found himself when writing this letter?

What might enable us to do this?

Reread: Philippians 2:29-30

What three things did Paul say should be characteristic of the way the Philippians welcomed Epaphroditus back? Please make a list.

1.

2.

3.

Why, in particular, do you think they were to treat him in this fashion?

How might it have impacted Epaphroditus to be welcomed back in this way?

How might it have impacted the people welcoming Epahproditus back if they did so properly?

How would it have impacted them individually?

How might it have impacted them as an ongoing fellowship group of believers?

Why, in your own words, was Paul able to count on Timothy and Epaphroditus? Please make a list.

1.

2.

3.

4.

5.

6.

7.

Among your believing friends, for whom do you have the highest regard? Why?

What risks are you willing to take on behalf of others who have trusted Jesus in a personal way?

In what ways do you feel you have been a reliable servant of God?

Application Questions

How can you be a model of humility and service to other believers this week?

Assuming that your relationship with God through Jesus is a solid one, how do you want people to react when you die?

Close in Prayer

WHAT REALLY COUNTS
PHILIPPIANS 3:1-11

Open in Prayer

Group Warm-Up Questions

If you were to update your resume' today, what recent accomplishments would you want to include?

How do you feel and respond when someone is better than you at something you do well?

Read: Philippians 3:1-11

Reread: Philippians 3:1

What did Paul tell the believers in Philippi to do?

Under what circumstances did he say that God wants us to do this?

Why did Paul never get tired of telling the believers to act in this way?

What is the expected result of following the admonition of Scripture to "be joyful in all circumstances?"

What is the difference between being joyful in all circumstances and being joyful for all circumstances?

Read:

1 Thessalonians 5:16-22

Philippians 4:4-7

Luke 2:10-11

John 15:11

John 17:13

How do these passages relate to what God is telling us in Philippians 3:1?

What is the practical result in one's life if they follow the clear direction of God's Word in this matter?

Let us digress for a moment and examine briefly the difference between happiness and joy.

Happiness is the English translation of the Latin word *fortuna*. The English word "fortune" and the expression "good fortune" as well as the words "fortunate" and "unfortunate" emanate from this root. It is easy for us to see that this assumes an element of chance tied to circumstances. Happiness is therefore circumstantial and dependent upon what is happening in one's life at the time.

Joy, however, is not circumstantial at all. It comes from within and is not dependent upon what is going on in one's life at the time. In its most pure sense joy is a supernatural inner quality springing from one's relationship with God. Some would define this as a supernatural inner quality of delight in God.

How then, does one obtain this joy?

There seem to be a number of components according to the Word of God. They include:

1. Trusting in Yeshua Ha-Maschiach, the Jewish Messiah, who we commonly call Jesus Christ on a personal basis. We see this in:

    • John 10:10.

2. Obtaining a holistic and mature knowledge of God's Word. This can be seen in:

    • Psalm 19:8.

    • Psalm 119:14.

    • John 15:10-11.

3. Pursuing a life pleasing to God of righteousness and peace. This is evident in:

    • Romans 14:17.

    • Philippians 4:6-7.

4. Realizing and obeying the essential command in God's Word to take advantage of this joy by adopting the necessary practices to obtain it in one's life on an ongoing basis. We see this in:

    • 1 Thessalonians 5:16-22 as previously noted.

Reread: Philippians 3:2

Against whom did Paul say the Philippians should be on guard?

In what four ways did Paul describe these people? Please make a list.

1.

2.

3.

4.

Note: Paul called these people "dogs." In the parlance of the day this was extremely derogatory. At the time Paul wrote this letter orthodox Jews referred to Gentiles as dogs, which were to them unclean animals. However, in this instance, Paul is actually applying this label to some orthodox Jews themselves. He is not, as Chuck Missler says, "just calling names: he is comparing these false teachers to the contemptible scavengers."

We must remember:

1. The Gospel was sent first to the Jews and came through them. See:

   • Acts 3:26.

   • Romans 1:16.

2. There was quite an uproar when Peter was called to make the Good News of Jesus available to the Gentiles. See:

   • Acts 15.

3. Paul was specifically called to take the message of life to the Gentiles. See:

   • Acts 13:1-3.

- Acts 22:21.

4. The dissenters, called the Judaizers, followed Paul everywhere. See:

  - The whole of the book of Acts.

5. The Judaizers incorrectly taught that one must be circumcised to experience life as a believer. See:

  - Acts 15:1.

  - Galatians 6:12-18.

6. The Judaizers missed the prophesized availability of the Gospel to the Gentiles. See:

  - Ephesians 2:8-9.

  - Titus 3:3-7.

Note: Errors such as the one in which the Judaizers fell into can be avoided by meticulously searching and applying the Word of God. See "How to Avoid Error" in the appendices at the back of this book for succinct and helpful details.

Reread: Philippians 3:3

Who did Paul say is truly circumcised?

What characteristics does he mention that are common to such people? He mentions three. Please enumerate them.

1.

2.

3.

Here we see Paul alluding to what is sometimes called circumcision of the heart. Read the following verses and note what we learn about this true circumcision.

Deuteronomy 30:6

Colossians 2:11-13

Romans 2:29

Genesis 15:6

Jeremiah 9:25

Galatians 5:6

Galatians 6:15

Colossians 3:11

Romans 4:9

Romans 3:30

Paul was perhaps the most highly educated and intelligent man of his day.

Read the following verses and please list what we learn about him as you go along.

Philippians 3:4-6

Acts 22:3 (Gamaliel was the preeminent Jewish teacher at the time of Paul's training.)

Galatians 1:13-14

    1.

    2.

    3.

    4.

    5.

    6.

    7.

    8.

9.

10.

11.

12.

13.

14.

15.

This is quite a list.

At what time and place did Paul say he was accused of violating any of the 613 commandments found in the Tanakh? (The Tanakh is what Jews call the Old Testament.)

Have you, at any point in your life, ever found that you had not acted in accordance with God's standard? (And hopefully rectified the situation.)

What are your thoughts about Paul knowing that the hypercritical and observant Pharisees had never accused him of violating any portion of the law?

Note 1: While it may not mean much to us today, Paul came from the tribe of Benjamin. At the time this would have been a source of pride for many people.

Israel's first king came from the tribe of Benjamin. And, the tribe of Benjamin was the only one to remain loyal to Judah when civil war divided Judah from Israel after the death of Solomon.

Note 2: Paul was a member of the Pharisees. This was regarded as the most faithful of the Jewish sects in their knowledge of and adherence to the law and the 613 commandments found therein. Being a member of the Pharisees was regarded as the summit of religious experience and office in Jewish culture at the time.

Note 3: Paul said he was a "real Hebrew," which is differentiated in the New Testament from a "true Jew." A real Hebrew was an ethnic Jew who evidenced all of the characteristics Paul noted exclusive of the persecution of believers.

A "true Jew" which he discusses in Romans 9 and Romans 2:28-29 is an ethnic Jew who has realized that Yeshua Ha-Maschiach, Jesus Christ, is the Jewish Messiah and has trusted Him on a personal basis.

Obviously, Paul was both.

In the autobiographical verses we previously read about Paul he evinced that his resume' was the most outstanding of any personage of his day.

Now read Philippians 3:7-9.

In what sense was Paul not boasting when he reviewed his accomplishments and qualifications?

How did he view his worldly achievements?

What did Paul say was of infinite value to him?

In what way did Paul say he had become truly righteous?

Upon what did Paul becoming truly righteous depend?

One is reminded of Paul Anderson, the world's strongest man. He set a weightlifting record several decades ago that has never been broken or even approached when he lifted 6,270 pounds off of railroad trestles.

Paul became a believer, started a home for troubled boys headed for prison, and traveled the world speaking and giving exhibitions of strength. Each time he spoke, his remarks included something like what the Paul of the New Testament said. Paul Anderson would commonly say in his booming voice: "They call me the strongest man in the world. I am an Olympic champion, a national champion, and a world champion, but the greatest thing in my life is to know Jesus Christ. I can't make it through a day without Him."

How does it impact you when you read and hear about the two Pauls and their faith?

How do you think hearing about the accomplishments and faith of these two followers of the Jewish Messiah impacts other people?

What kinds of things do people normally boast about?

What kinds of things do you normally boast about?

How is your recitation of your accomplishments like or unlike that of Saul of Tarsus (Paul) and Paul Anderson?

Reread: Philippians 3:8

Why do you think Paul referred to all of his worldly achievements as "garbage?" Please explain what this means to you.

Why do people sometimes tend to base their estimation of their worth as believers on their accomplishments?

In what should believers find their identity and confidence?

Read:

Romans 12:2

2 Timothy 3:16-17

Ephesians 5:18

By what processes can believers come to the place of correctly finding their identity and confidence?

Reread: Philippians 3:9

What was Paul's status as a believer?

As an interesting aside we might note that the book of Romans elaborates on three ways human beings attempt to rationalize their behavior and claim an undeserved spot in the kingdom of God. This includes those who are:

1. Self-justified. This is seen in Romans 1:18-22 and indicted in:

    •   Romans 1:21-28.

2. Moral. This is seen in Romans 2:1-16 and indicted in:

   • Romans 3:23.

3. Religious. This is evident in Romans 2:17-29 and indicted in:

   • 1 Samuel 16:7.

Based upon your reading of Philippians 3:9, do you feel that having faith is an instantaneous event or the result of a path of growth? Please explain.

Reread: Philippians 3:10-11

Also read: Romans 6:4

Again, The Holy Spirit has packed a lot of information in these verses. Please list the component parts of what had become Paul's desire.

   1.

   2.

   3.

   4.

   5.

   6.

   7.

Read: Galatians 2:20

Some people say that this verse summarizes Paul's position on a spiritual basis. What do you think? Please explain.

Note: The Greek word used for knowing Jesus or fellowship with Him in verse 10 is *koinonia*. Use of this word indicates a sense of partnership and participation. In the case of Paul, he exchanged a set of 613 rules for a relationship with Jesus as his Master, Companion, Friend, and Lord all at the same time.

Verse 10 also mentions suffering. Strangely enough it often seems that one's relationship with God becomes stronger and more intimate through suffering. How might you explain this?

For further information on the topic of faith and suffering I suggest that a member of the group read and present a ten minute book report on *Faith in the Night Seasons* by Nancy Missler.

Application Questions

Is there anything in your life you ought to count as "rubbish" for the sake of your relationship with God? Please explain.

What specific accomplishments in your life can be used to point people toward a personal relationship with Jesus Christ?

Close in Prayer

WEEK 7

THE BEST CITIZENSHIP
PHILIPPIANS 3:12-4:1

Open in Prayer

Group Warm-Up Questions

Do you spend more time watching or participating in sports or physical activities? Why?

If you lived several thousand years ago and had the choice of participating in sports as either a javelin thrower or a chariot racer, which would you pick? Why?

Read: Philippians 3:12-4:1

Reread: Philippians 3:12

Did Paul, who was quite accomplished in most areas of life, feel that he had reached perfection?

What was Paul's life goal in attitude and conduct?

How does he relate this goal to his relationship with Jesus, the Jewish Messiah?

What do you think it means that Jesus "possessed him for perfection when He first possessed him?"

Read: Romans 8:28

How does this apply to those who have made a decision to follow Jesus in today's world? Please explain.

Assuming that you are a believer, how does this apply to you?

Reread: Philippians 3:13

Also read: Luke 9:62

Note: Examining the meaning of the original language in this verse we find that the concept translated as "forget" does not mean "to fail to remember."

What mental process does Paul employ in his effort to be what God intends him to be?

How might this have been helpful to him?

How might this be helpful to people today?

What kind of particular things in one's past might one do well to "forget?"

Does this mean that they are erased from our memories or that our focus has changed?

Does this "forgetting" mean that we should ignore the lessons we have learned from experiences of the past?

Note: In particular, these verses, taken with the whole of Scripture, seem to indicate that we should not focus on the negative, destructive and harmful events and thoughts in our past. Conversely, the whole of Scripture indicates that we are to focus on other things.

Read: Philippians 4:8

According to this verse, what sort of things ought a believer to focus upon in order to live a successful life?

Note: We should also realize that psychologists tell us the human brain works in such a fashion that the best way to eliminate negative thought patterns is to simply replace them with new and positive thought patterns. Thus, simply trying to not think about "wrong" things that are harmful to us is not enough. In fact, overtly attempting to not focus on certain things actually causes us to focus on them. Instead, we must purposefully focus on things that are helpful.

Read: Ephesians 4:29-30

How do these verses help us understand the positive utility of this concept as it relates to our lives and the lives of others?

Thankfully, believers do not have to do this all on their own. We have the power of the Holy Spirit to assist us. Please read the following verses and discuss how this seems to work.

Galatians 5:22-23

Romans 12:2

While remembering past successes can be motivational and inspiring to us, can doing so actually impede progress in our spiritual race if we permit it to lead us to inaction by "resting on our laurels?"

Can you think of a time when you have seen or heard of an athlete doing this? Please describe the situation.

Conversely, can you think of a time when you have seen an athlete or anyone else use past successes as a positive tool toward greater accomplishments? Please explain.

Have you seen these principles operating in your life? How so?

Reread: Philippians 3:13

Thus far we have primarily discussed the principle of not focusing on the past in a negative way in this verse. Now let us turn our attention to the second principle of focusing on what lies ahead.

In particular, we might do well to concentrate on the principle of a laser-like focus on what matters most. Read the following verses and discuss what that one thing is in the life of a victorious believer:

Mark 10:21

Luke 10:42

John 9:25

Psalm 27:4

Ben Franklin is often quoted as having said that a person might best succeed by being a generalist when he supposedly quipped "Jack of all trades and master of none." Interestingly, this is an incorrect quote. He actually said that one must be a "Jack of all trades and master of ONE."

What is the difference between these two concepts as you see it?

Might the Judeo Christian Scriptures, which we today call the Bible, be that "one" irreplaceable and necessary ingredient for a life worth living? How so?

Finally, we might point out that the words translated "looking forward" or "reaching forth," depending upon which version of the Bible you are using, literally mean "stretching as in a race."

How does this stretching forth toward victory translate to life, thoughts, and action in the world of a believer?

Reread: Philippians 3:14

Also read: 1 Corinthians 9:24-27

How does Paul summarize his application of the principles we have so far discussed today?

How might we do the same in practical terms in our lives today? Please make a list.

1.

2.

3.

4.

5.

6.

7.

How might you summarize Paul's overall life goal from what we read in Philippians 3:14?

What is your overall life goal?

Note: There are two out of context extremes against which we must guard:

1. Assuming that God will do all the work in the world and we have to do nothing but sit back and watch. This attitude is sometimes characterized by someone blindingly accepting a situation and saying "it must be the will of God."

2. Assuming that God wants us to "be His hands and feet" and do all of the work on our own.

These misconceptions can be avoided by a careful application of the truths found throughout God's Word and particularly in:

- Philippians 2:12

- John 15:5

- Philippians 2:13

- 1 Timothy 4:7-8

Going back to the time Philippians was written we might further note that in order to participate in the Greek athletic games one had to be a citizen. How does this translate to a believer's "citizenship" and striving for perfection? Please explain.

Reread: Philippians 3:15

What was Paul's hope for spiritually mature believers in terms of the focus of their thoughts and actions?

By what methodology does God make such principles clear to believers?

Read the following verses and enumerate the necessary components of this process.

1 Thessalonians 5:16-22

Matthew 4:4

John 7:38-39

John 14:6

John 14:26

Isaiah 55:11

Romans 12:1-2

Colossians 3:23-24

Philippians 4:8-9

Psalm 1:1-2

John 17:17

1.

2.

3.

4.

5.

Reread: Philippians 3:16

What important practice does Paul put forth in this verse?

How does focusing our thoughts on the positive activities and results we have seen in our lives thus far help us?

Reread: Philippians 3:17

In what way did Paul encourage the Philippians to learn from his life and those who were already emulating him?

How does this type of thing work out in real practice in life today? Please give an example.

Read:

James 3:1

2 Timothy 2:24

Romans 15:14

Luke 6:40

1 Peter 3:15

2 Timothy 3:16-17

Ephesians 4:11-12

Matthew 28:19-20

What special responsibility does this process place upon teachers and leaders?

How can you follow Paul's example in your life today?

Reread: Philippians 3:18

What disgraceful thing did Paul see happening in the lives of some people who professed to follow God in his day?

Do we still see this happening in the world today? How so?

What does one's conduct show about their relationship to Jesus?

Reread: Philippians 3:19

What kinds of things do people who are "Christians" in name only but whose conduct indicates differently focus on?

What is the end result of this lifestyle?

What kind of opposition do you personally face as you strive to live your life in accordance with God's clear standards? Please describe and discuss.

Reread: Philippians 3:20

What citizenship is of prime importance to believers?

From the introduction to the book of Philippians we might recall that Roman citizenship has special significance to the people living in Philippi.

Roman citizenship in that era and in the Roman Empire carried with it great prestige, privilege and honor. This included:

- Exemption from floggings and arrest (except in extreme cases).

- Exemption from the death penalty unless guilty of treason.

- Exemption from paying tribute to Caesar unlike the taxes imposed on most foreign conquered lands.

- The right to acquire, hold, and transfer land.

- The right of self-government to regulate civic affairs on a corporate basis.

- The attendant rights to vote in assemblies and stand for civil or public office.

- The right to make legal contracts.

- The right to sue and be sued in the courts and have a legal trial.

- The right to appeal directly to Caesar.

- An exclusive position as it is estimated that only 15% of the citizens of the Roman controlled world were Roman citizens.

In many ways citizenship in heaven is referenced in Scripture. Read the following verses to see what we learn:

John 3:3

Matthew 3:2

Matthew 7:21

Romans 14:17

Romans 8:19

1 John 2:15-17

Matthew 6:19-20

2 Corinthians 5:17

Ephesians 2:18-19

Hebrews 11:10, 13-16

In what way might the privileges of Roman citizenship relate to the citizenship a believer enjoys?

Reread: Philippians 3:20

Note: A believer's citizenship in heaven is spoken of in the present tense, not only as some anticipated future event. How does this make you feel?

Larry Norman, the "Father of Christian Rock and Roll," thought of himself as a citizen of heaven. Two of his most popular albums were entitled *Only Visiting This Planet* and *In Another Land*. What might these titles convey to someone?

When you see a citizen from another country visiting yours, how can you tell they are from another land?

If a believer currently has citizenship in heaven, what evidence should we see of it in their life? Please explain and expound making a list. First, however, read:

Colossians 4:5-6

Ephesians 4:29-30

1 Peter 3:15

Galatians 5:22-23

1.

2.

3.

4.

5.

6.

7.

If you are a believer and have trusted Jesus on a personal basis, is your citizenship in heaven evident in your life? How so?

Reread: Philippians 3:21

Also read: 1 John 3:2

To what do all believers look forward when Jesus returns?

Is this promised future change attractive to you?

How, in your particular situation, does this promised future change to your body impact you? Why?

What, in addition to the changes believers will experience on a personal level, will also occur when Jesus Christ, the Jewish Messiah, returns?

Reread: Philippians 4:1

What does God command believers to do prior to the return of Jesus?

Note: The words translated "stand fast" or "stay true to the Lord," depending upon which version of the Bible you are reading, are actually military terms in the original language. Their literal meaning is to *hold the ground that has been conquered.*

Ephesians 6:11-14 says:

11 Put on all of God's armor so that you will be able to stand firm against all strategies of the devil. 12 For we are not fighting against flesh-and-blood enemies, but against evil rulers and authorities of the unseen world, against mighty powers in this dark world, and against evil spirits in the heavenly places. 13 Therefore, put on every piece of God's armor so you will be able to resist the enemy in the time of evil. Then after the battle you will still be standing firm. 14 Stand your ground, putting on the belt of truth and the body armor of God's righteousness. (NLT)

What additional insight does understanding of the original language in concert with what we see in the above excerpt from Ephesians give you into the responsibility of a believer in everyday life? Please explain.

How did Paul feel about the Philippian believers to whom he addressed this letter?

In what way were the believers in Philippi Paul's "joy and crown?"

Is it possible for a committed believing teacher to feel this way about those they have taught in today's world? How so?

Please explain how you might see this working out in actual practice.

Application Question

In the Scripture under consideration today the life of a believer is likened to running a race. In what spiritual workouts or training will you engage this week to win this race?

Close in Prayer

GOD'S FORMULA FOR MENTAL HEALTH AND PEACE
PHILIPPIANS 4:2-9

Open in Prayer

Group Warm-Up Questions

What does it take to live with difficult family members or colleagues?

How do you tend to respond when things don't go your way?

Read: Philippians 4:1-9

Reread: Philippians 4:1

What did Paul so earnestly want the believers in Philippi to do?

Why was this so important to him?

Reread: Philippians 4:2

For what two people in Philippi did Paul have a particular concern?

What seems to have been the problem between these two women?

Reread: Philippians 4:3

First, let's attempt to clear up a mystery.

People have often wondered about the identity of Paul's "true partner" mentioned in this verse. We should note that in the original language the masculine form of the noun is used so we know that he is referring to a man.

Read Philippians 2:25 and see if you think Epaphroditus fits the bill in this particular situation. Please explain your conclusion and reasoning.

What had Euodia and Syntyche done when working together with Paul? Please make a short list.

1.

2.

3.

4.

5.

How do you imagine these two women came to the place where they had such a difficult disagreement?

What do you think they may have been "fighting" over?

Note: Paul seems to regard whatever they were struggling with to be inconsequential.

Have you seen a situation like this where:

1. Two good people get caught up in an inconsequential disagreement?

2. The contention is an impediment to both of them?

3. The contention itself is harmful to the people around them?

4. The negative emotional environment created is detrimental to the group as a whole?

Please give an example.

How was this problem addressed either with or without success?

In your opinion, why do things like this occur?

Note: At this point we should realize that this particular issue is being addressed in the verses that follow and that we are examining today. God has provided us with specific practical and effective ways to deal with such situations.

Reread: Philippians 4:4-6

In these verses we are provided with a partial solution to the type of contention exhibited between these two women. Paul has, in fact, given us a portion of a formula with very specific ingredients. Please list what you see in these few verses below.

1.

2.

3.

4.

5.

6.

7.

Having extracted this list from God's Word, please go back over it and discuss why each item is important and how it works in the life of a believer.

If these things work so effectively in the individual lives of believers, how then do they impact the group of believers to whom they belong? Please think of as many as you can.

In what other areas of life might these principles be helpful? Please name a few.

Why is this so?

Which ingredient on this list is mentioned with double force?

Why do you think it is mentioned in that way?

One might assume that it is of particular power and importance. Please explain why this might be so.

Reread: Philippians 4:4

Note: For some people it is a stark realization that this verse indicates experiencing joy is a choice.

The Merriam Webster dictionary defines joy as "the emotion evoked by well-being, success, or good fortune or by the prospect of possessing what one desires."

This joy comes from within a person and can be kindled or extinguished based upon what is happening in the heart, mind, and spirit of someone.

While happiness is somewhat related, the feeling of contentment and well-being associated with it is based upon external circumstances alone and one's response to them.

Strangely, then, it is possible for a person to be joyful without being happy or happy without being joyful.

Knowing that joy is a choice, how do people in the world today attempt to achieve joy on their own?

Read:

1Thessalonians 5:16-22

Galatians 5:22-23.

2 Timothy 3:16-17

According to these verses, in what way can a believer experience true joy in the midst of the trials and tribulations of life?

Please explain how the concepts in these three references work together to make joy a reality in the life of a believer. (The answer to this question is not a short one.)

How it is possible for someone to be joyful and not happy? Please cite an example.

Conversely, how it is possible for someone to be happy but not joyful? Please give an example.

Reread: Philippians 4:6

In the world, many people characterize themselves as "worrywarts." What do they mean by this?

Over five hundred years ago Michel de Montaigne said "My life has been filled with terrible misfortune, most of which never happened." More recently, Don Joseph Goewey, author of *The End of Stress,* claimed that in the subjects he studied, 85% of what people worry about never happened. Furthermore, he found that when things people worry about do happen they turn out much better than they feared 79% of the time.

This would indicate that 97% of what people worry about is nothing more than a fearful mind running amuck, irrationally catastrophizing things. While this may be statistically true, worry remains a terrible problem for many people. People in the field of psychology and counseling say that it can cause family dysfunction and can lead to marital problems, and depression.

On top of that, researchers in the field of medicine claim it actually promotes premature aging, shrinks brain mass, lowers one's IQ, and can contribute to Alzheimer's disease and dementia.

Why then is worry such a problem to many people in the world today?

Chuck Missler, speaking of worry, said: "Worry is a trickle of fear passing through the mind which soon cuts a crevice so deep that it drains all other thoughts away."

According to the following verses, believers do not need to worry. They would be remiss to not plan, but worrying is destructive, wrong, and in fact, disobedient. Please read the following verses and note what we learn about worry, trust, planning, and love.

Romans 8:28

Romans 12:2

1 John 4:18

Matthew 6:25-34

Matthew 11:28-30

Proverbs 22:5

Proverbs 24:27

Proverbs 3:5-6

Luke 14:28

Proverbs 15:22

Proverbs 21:5

Psalm 127:1

Psalm 119:105

Proverbs 3:9

Proverbs 23:23-27

James 4:13-17

Matthew 6:33

James 1:5

2 Timothy 1:7

Reread: Philippians 4:7

What great promise do we have if we follow the formula God provides to us in Philippians 4:4-6?

What does this great peace do specifically?

In what way does it guard our hearts and minds? How do you see this working?

Can you think of an example when you have followed these principles with the promised result in your life? Please explain.

Reread: Philippians 4:8

As if God has not already provided us with enough tools for life, here He provides us with yet another key ingredient. How would you put the admonitions in this verse in your own words?

Note: Psychologists tell us that the principle in this verse is more powerful than we might imagine. According to them, the way to get rid of negative thoughts and their consequences is NOT to try and not focus on them. The result of such an effort is that we end up focusing on the things we do not want to think about with destructive results in our minds, hearts and lives.

However, if we follow the Scriptural principle in Philippians 4:8 we can, in fact, effectively counteract and extinguish negative thoughts and their resultant consequences. The human brain can most effectively eliminate harmful thoughts and tendencies by replacing them with good things. This then vastly improves the qualities of ones thought patterns and life as a whole.

It took psychologists a long time to figure this out.

Believers adhering to the Word of God have been privileged to know it and experience it for thousands of years.

Suggestion: Memorizing Scripture is a powerful tool in the lives of those who do it. I suggest that everyone memorize Philippians 4:8 and enjoy testing each other on it the next time the group convenes. If anyone is feeling really ambitious perhaps they can memorize Philippians 4:4-8.

Reread: Philippians 4:9

What else does Paul tell the believers in Philippi to do?

Note: We would do well to remember the circumstances in which Paul found himself when he wrote this letter to the Philippians. He was imprisoned and could have been executed any day. Yet he seems unconcerned for his own well-being. He is writing to tell the Philippians, who were not in prison and facing the daily possibility of execution, that they should not worry and follow his example and the formula God has provided. For him to tell them to follow his example was not a hollow claim or a boast of any sort. It was founded in fact and his heartfelt desire for the Philippian believers to enjoy the fullness of life found through the Jewish Messiah. (See John 10:10)

How does it help people when they have a positive role model in front of them?

How is it harmful when we see negative role models?

Why do role models have such an impact?

Application Questions

In what circumstance can you be the kind of positive role model God desires this coming week? Please think of a specific situation.

How can you apply the formula we find in today's Scripture references for healthy relationships and personal inner peace to your life this week?

Close in Prayer

SECRETS OF CONTENTMENT
PHILIPPIANS 4:10-23

Open in Prayer

Group Warm-Up Questions

When was a time you experienced contentment in the middle of problems or uncertainty? Please explain.

What experiences bring you the most contentment?

Test

In our last session we discussed the many benefits of memorizing Scripture. We challenged the members of our group to memorize Philippians 4:8 or Philippians 4:4-8 if they were feeling more adventurous. At this point I suggest the progress of those doing the memorization be tested and a small, appropriate and enjoyable award be given to those who made the effort.

Read: Philippians 4:10-23

Reread: Philippians 4:10

Why was Paul glad?

What understanding does Paul have about the situation of the Philippians?

Reread: Philippians 4:11

When did Paul consider himself to be in need?

Why did he feel this way?

Do you feel the same way Paul did or do you have a different experience? Please elaborate.

Reread: Philippians 4:12

How did Paul elaborate on what he had learned? There are seven parts to this concept mentioned. Please list them.

    1.

    2.

    3.

    4.

    5.

    6.

    7.

From your study of the Scriptures you may know that seven is the biblical number of completion. We also know that nothing is in God's Word by accident. Why, then, do you imagine that there are seven parts to this concept?

How can you apply these principles in your life today?

Reread: Philippians 4:13

How does this verse further explain the concept in Philippians 4:12?

Note: This verse has often been taken out of context. Sometimes this is done by Christian athletes who feel it gives them the ability and license to believe that they can accomplish any athletic feat. It is easy to see why someone might take this verse in that fashion. In fact, it is easy to see why this verse has been inspirational to many people. Please explain how this verse might be used in life situations in a positive fashion knowing the original context.

How do you handle the unexpected?

Read: John 15:1-5

What important truth is brought home in these verses if we are to effectively claim the promise in Philippians 4:13?

Note: Hudson Taylor was a great missionary to China. For many years he worked hard but found no joy or freedom in his ministry. He received a letter from a friend who helped him understand the crucial error he had been making. He was, humanly speaking, an incredibly faithful man. However, he had been relying on his own not insubstantial work and discipline for success, joy, and happiness. In his own words he summed up what he had to do to experience success and joy in his life when he said, "It is not by trusting my own faithfulness, but by looking away to the Faithful One!"

Note: Most any believer will benefit by taking the time to read *Hudson Taylor's Spiritual Secret* by Dr. and Mrs. Howard Taylor. I suggest that one of the members of the group volunteer to read and present a 5-10 minute report on this book at the next study session.

Philippians 4:14

What did the Philippians do when they knew Paul needed help?

How did Paul feel toward the Philippians even though he already knew the secret of contentment?

Why did he feel this way even though he was content?

Does this happen to people in the same way today? How so?

Reread: Philippians 4:15-16

How had the Philippians helped Paul?

Why do you think they helped him even when he was apart from them and telling other groups the Good News about the Jewish Messiah?

Who else helped Paul when he came to see the Philippians and then traveled on to Macedonia?

Why do you think the Philippians, and only the Philippians, helped him at this point in time?

Does this sort of thing still happen in the world today?

Why is it that the action of only one committed person or group among thousands so often makes a difference for good or bad? Please explain.

Interestingly, God's Word has a lot to say about this concept as it relates to those who follow Him.

Read:

Proverbs 2:20

Proverbs 3:3

Proverbs 3:5-6

Proverbs 3:27

Proverbs 8:13

Proverbs 8:7

Proverbs 10:32

Proverbs 11:25

Proverbs 11:30

Proverbs 14:25

Proverbs 14:31

Proverbs 16:11

Proverbs 17:15

Proverbs 17:17

Proverbs 18:4

Proverbs 18:24

Proverbs 21:15

Proverbs 25:26

Proverbs 27:10

Deuteronomy 24:17

Deuteronomy 27:19

Isaiah 58:6

Psalm 82:3

Matthew 5:14-16

Amos 5:14-15

James 1:27

Isaiah 1:17

Proverbs 31:8-9

Proverbs 24:11-12

Matthew 5:14-16

What should a believer do when he or she has it within their power to have a positive impact upon a situation?

Have you ever done this? Please give an example.

Reread: Philippians 4:17

What was Paul not asking for?

Conversely, what did he most earnestly desire?

Why do you think he wanted to see this?

Does this seem to work itself out in the world today? How so?

Reread: Philippians 4:18

What was Paul's financial situation at the time?

How does God regard our gifts for His work?

Reread: Philippians 4:19

What great promise do believers have?

Is this promise some sort of reciprocal agreement with God contingent upon "our" gifts to Him, as some people claim? Please explain.

What exactly do you take Philippians 4:19 to mean? Remember, there are believers in the world being tortured and killed for their faith as you read these words.

Read: Philippians 4:6-7

Does this verse somehow tie in with Philippians 4:19? Please explain.

How do these concepts tie in with Paul's situation at the time he wrote this letter? Remember, he was in prison and his life could have been forfeited any day. In fact, he could have been executed even as the ink dried on his letter.

Reread: Philippians 4:20

What did Paul do in spite of the precarious situation in which he found himself?

How do you think he was he able to do this with sincerity?

Reread: Philippians 4:21-22

To whom did Paul send final greetings?

Who else joined him in sending these wishes?

This seems to infer that the believers in Rome were supporting each other even though they were living in "enemy territory."

How does this relate to believers today? What can we learn from it?

Speaking of the believers in Caesar's household we should remember that Paul was in the custody of the Praetorian Guards and as such was normally chained to one of them. These elite soldiers would have been listening to and talking with Paul for hours on end each day. Do you think some of them were numbered among the believers in Caesar's household who were sending greetings to the believers in Philippi? Why or why not?

Reread: Philippians 4:23

What final wish did Paul have for the Philippians?

Why do you think he closed his letter in this fashion?

Application Questions

What can you do this week to help a fellow believer who needs financial assistance, assuming it is in your power to do something?

What person do you know who needs a written note of encouragement from you today?

What can you do to develop the attitude of contentment in all circumstances, applying the principles used by Paul? Please explain the specific steps you will take.

Close in Prayer

APPENDIX 1

HOW TO AVOID ERROR
(PARTIALLY EXCERPTED FROM *THE ROAD TO HOLOCAUST* BY HAL LINDSEY)

1. The most important single principle in determining the true meaning of any doctrine of our faith is that we start with the clear statements of the Scriptures that specifically apply to it, and use those to interpret the parables, allegories and obscure passages. This allows Scripture to interpret Scripture. The Dominionists (and others seeking to bend Scripture to suit their purposes) frequently reverse this order, seeking to interpret the clear passages using obscure passages, parables and allegories.

2. The second most important principle is to consistently interpret by the literal, grammatical, historical method. This means the following:

   1. Each word should be interpreted in light of its normal, ordinary usage that was accepted in the times in which it was written.

   2. Each sentence should be interpreted according to the rules of grammar and syntax normally accepted when the document was written.

   3. Each passage should also be interpreted in light of its historical and cultural environment.

Most false doctrines and heresy of Church history can be traced to a failure to adhere to these principles. Church history is filled with examples of disasters and wrecked lives wrought by men failing to base their doctrine, faith, and practice upon these two principles.

The Reformation, more than anything else, was caused by an embracing of the literal, grammatical, and historical method of interpretation, and a discarding of the allegorical method. The allegorical system had veiled the Church's understanding of many vital truths for nearly a thousand years.

Note 1: It is important to note that this is how Jesus interpreted Scripture. He interpreted literally, grammatically, and recognized double reference in prophecy.

Note 2: It is likewise important that we view Scripture as a whole. Everything we read in God's Word is part of a cohesive, consistent, integrated message system. Every part of Scripture fits in perfectly with the whole of Scripture if we read, understand, and study it properly.

Note 3: Remember to appropriate the power of The Holy Spirit.

Read: Luke 11:11-13
Read: Luke 24:49
Read: John 7:38-39
Read: John 14:14-17, 26

Read: 1 Timothy 4:15-16
Read: 2 Peter 2:1
Read: Mark 13:22

APPENDIX 2

UNDERSTANDING COMPOSITE PROBABILITY AND APPLYING IT TO THE JUDEO-CHRISTIAN SCRIPTURES

Before proceeding we might briefly reflect upon the reliability of the Judeo-Christian Scriptures. All honest researchers into their veracity have found that, as historical documents, they are without parallel. They are the most reliable and incontrovertibly accurate documents available in the world today. This has been the conclusion of all the erudite scholars and investigators who have taken the time to delve into this topic. For more information on this subject you may wish to read *The Case For Christ* by Lee Stroebel, *More Than a Carpenter* by Josh McDowell, and the *Evidence That Demands a Verdict* series, also by Josh McDowell. This is, of course, a very short list of the volumes available. A great deal of augmentative and corroborative material is available in such volume that if one were so inclined they might spend a lifetime in its study.

To better understand one of the ways the Creator of the Universe has validated His Word and the work and person of Jesus Christ, it is helpful to get a grasp on composite probability theory and its application to the Judeo-Christian Scriptures.

We are indebted to Peter W. Stoner, past chairman of the Department of Mathematics and Astronomy at Pasadena City College as well as to Dr. Robert C. Newman with his Ph.D. in astrophysics from Cornell University for the initial statistical work on this topic. Their joint efforts on composite probability theory were first published in the book *Science Speaks.*

Composite Probability Theory

If something has a 1 in 10 chance of occurring, that is easy for us to understand. It means that 10 percent of the time, the event will happen. However, when we calculate the probability of several different events occurring at the same time, the odds of that happening increase exponentially. This is the basic premise behind composite probability theory.

If two events have a 1 in 10 chance of happening, the chance that both of these events will occur is 1 in 10 x 10, or 1 in 100. To show this numerically this probability would be 1 in 10^2, with the superscript indicating how many tens are being multiplied. If we have 10^3, it means that we have a number of 1000. Thus 10^4 is equivalent to 10,000 and so on. This is referred to as 10 to the first power, 10 to the second power, 10 to the third power, and so on.

For example, let's assume that there are ten people in a room. If one of the ten is left handed and one of the ten has red hair, the probability that any one person in the room will be left handed and have red hair is one in one hundred.

We can apply this model to the prophecy revealed in the Bible to figure out the mathematical chances of Jesus' birth, life and death, in addition to many other events occurring in the New Testament by chance. To demonstrate this, we will consider eight prophecies about Jesus and assign a probability of them occurring individually by chance. To eliminate any disagreement, we will be much more limiting than is necessary. Furthermore, we will use the prophecies that are arguably the most unlikely to be fulfilled by chance. I think you will agree that in doing so, we are severely handicapping ourselves.

1. The first prophecy from Micah 5:2 says, "But you, O Bethlehem Ephrathah, are only a small village in Judah. Yet a ruler of Israel will come from you, one whose origins are from the distant past" (NLT). This prophecy tells us that the Messiah will be born in Bethlehem. What is the chance of that actually occurring? As we consider this, we also have to ask: What is the probability that anyone in the history of the world might be born in this obscure town? When we take into account all of the people who ever lived, this might conservatively be 1 in 200,000.

Amazingly, about 700 years after this prophecy was uttered it was fulfilled when Yeshua HaMaschiach (The Jewish Messiah), who we call Jesus, was born in exactly the place predicted. We see this in Luke 2:11 where it states "The Savior— yes, the Messiah, the Lord—has been born today in Bethlehem, the city of David!"

2. Let's move on to the second prophecy in Zechariah 9:9: "Rejoice greatly, O people of Zion! Shout in triumph, O people of Jerusalem! Look, your King is coming to you. He is righteous and victorious, yet He is humble, riding on a donkey---even on a donkey's colt" (NLT). For our purposes, we can assume the chance that the Messiah (the King) riding into Jerusalem on a donkey might be 1 in 100. But, really, how many kings in the history of the world have actually done this?

This fulfillment of this particular prophecy 500 years later was so unnerving that Matthew, Mark, Luke and John all included it in their historical accounts.

Matthew recorded it as "Tell the people of Jerusalem, 'Look, your King is coming to you. He is humble, riding on a donkey— riding on a donkey's colt' " (Matthew 21:5 NLT).

This appears in John's writings as "The next day, the news that Jesus was on the way to Jerusalem swept through the city. A large crowd of Passover visitors took palm branches and went down the road to meet him. They shouted, "Praise God! Blessings on the one who comes in the name of the Lord! Hail to the King of Israel!" Jesus found a young donkey and rode on it, fulfilling the prophecy that said: "Don't be afraid, people of Jerusalem. Look, your King is coming, riding on a donkey's colt" (John 12:12–15 NLT).

3. The third prophecy is from Zechariah 11:12: "I said to them, 'If you like, give me my wages, whatever I am worth; but only if you want to.' So they counted out for my wages thirty pieces of silver" (NLT). What is the chance that someone would be betrayed and the price of that betrayal would be thirty pieces of silver? For our purposes, let's assume the chance that anyone in the history of the world would be betrayed for thirty pieces of silver might be 1 in 1,000.

As unlikely as it may have seemed on the surface, this prediction was fulfilled approximately 500 years later and was noted by Matthew with the language itself being eerily similar to what had been written so many years ago. The NLT shows this as "How much will you pay me to betray Jesus to you? And they gave him thirty pieces of silver." (Matthew 26:15) How shocking would it be if you found that someone predicted exactly what you were going to spend for your next dinner out 500 years ago?

4. The fourth prophecy comes from Zechariah 11:13: "And the Lord said to me, 'Throw it to the potter'---this magnificent sum at which they valued me! So I took the thirty coins and threw them to the potter in the Temple of the Lord" (NLT). Now we need to consider what the chances would be that a temple and a potter would be involved in someone's betrayal. For our statistical model, let's assume this is 1 in 100,000.

This prophecy and its fulfillment is a continuation and completion of the one immediately prior to it in which the exact amount of the bribe for the betrayal of the Jewish King was predicted, again 500 years before it occurred. Here we find predicted not only the betrayal and the exact payment, but the actual usage of the funds. Matthew records fulfillment of this whole process as "I have sinned," he declared, "for I have betrayed an innocent man." "What do we care?" they retorted. "That's your problem." Then Judas threw the silver coins down in the Temple and went out and hanged himself. The leading priests picked up the coins. "It wouldn't be right to put this money in the Temple treasury," they said, "since it was payment for murder." After some discussion they finally decided to buy the potter's field, and they made it into a cemetery for foreigners (Matthew 27:4-7 NLT).

5. The fifth prophecy in Zechariah 13:6 reads: "And one shall say unto him, What are these wounds in thine hands? Then he shall answer, Those with which I was wounded in the house of my friends" (KJV). The question here is, "How many people in the history of the world have died with wounds in their hands?" I believe we can safely assume the chance of any person dying with wounds in his or her hands is somewhat greater than 1 in 1,000.

Again, 500 years later we see this specific prophecy fulfilled and the evidence viewed by Jesus' disciples in John 20:20 where it says "As he spoke, he showed them the wounds in his hands and his side. They were filled with joy when they saw the Lord" (NLT)!

6. The sixth prophecy in Isaiah 53:7 states, "He was oppressed and treated harshly, yet he never said a word. He was led like a lamb to the slaughter. And as a sheep is silent before the shearers, he did not open his mouth" (NLT). This raises a particularly tough question. How many people in the history of the world can we imagine being put on trial, knowing they were innocent, without making one statement in their defense? For our statistical model, let's say this is 1 in 1,000, although it is pretty hard to imagine.

In this case, approximately 700 years passed between the time the prediction was made and we see it fulfilled in Mark 15:3-5. There it is recorded as "Then the leading priests kept accusing him of many crimes, and Pilate asked him, "Aren't you going to answer them? What about all these charges they are bringing against you?" But Jesus said nothing, much to Pilate's surprise" (NLT).

7. Moving on to the seventh prophecy, Isaiah 53:9 says "He had done no wrong and had never deceived anyone. But he was buried like a criminal; he was put in a rich man's grave" (NLT). Here we need to consider how many people, out of all the good individuals in the world who have died, have died a criminal's death and been buried in a rich person's grave. These people died out of place. (Some might also infer that they were buried out of place, though that is not necessarily true.) Let's assume the chance of a good person dying as a criminal and being buried with the rich is about 1 in 1,000.

Again we find that 700 years passed between the prediction of this event and the actual occurrence. Again, this event was so momentous that it was recorded by Matthew, Mark, Luke and John. Astonishingly, we find that he was placed in the tomb by not just one person of wealth, but by two. Joseph of Arimathea and Nicodemus, two of the wealthiest men in the region, worked together and laid the body in Joseph's own tomb. Matthew 27:60, speaking of Joseph of Arimathea's part in entombing Jesus' body says "He placed it in his own new tomb, which had been carved out of the rock. Then he rolled a great stone across the entrance and left" (NLT).

8. The eighth and final prophecy is from Psalm 22:16: "My enemies surround me like a pack of dogs; an evil gang closes in on me. They have pierced my hands and feet" (NLT). Remember this passage and all the other prophetic references to the crucifixion were written before this form of execution was invented. However, for our purposes, we just need to consider the probability of someone in the history of the world being executed by crucifixion. Certainly, Jesus wasn't the only person killed by being crucified. We will say that the chances of a person dying from this specific form of execution to be at 1 in 10,000.

Here we might note that Psalm 22 was penned by King David approximately 1000 years prior to the birth of Jesus. The word "crucifixion" and its derivatives had not yet been coined, but we see the process described in detail. Again, because of the import of this event it is recorded by each of the Gospel writers. In Mark 16:6 we see the fulfillment of the ancient prophecy and more where we read "Don't be alarmed. You are looking for Jesus of Nazareth, who was crucified. He isn't here! He is risen from the dead! Look, this is where they laid his body" (NLT).

Calculating the Results

To determine the chance that all these things would happen to the same person by chance, we simply need to multiply the fraction of each of the eight probabilities. When we do, we get a chance of 1 in 10^{28}. In other words, the probability is 1 in 10,000,000,000,000,000,000,000,000,000.

Would you bet against these odds?

Unfortunately, there is another blow coming for those who do not believe the Bible is true or Jesus is who He said He was. There are not just eight prophecies of this nature in the Bible that were fulfilled in Jesus Christ------there are *more than three hundred* such prophecies in the Old Testament. The prophecies we looked at were just the ones that we could *most easily* show fulfilled.

If we deal with only forty-eight prophecies about Jesus, based on the above numbers, the chance that Jesus is not who He said He was or the Bible is not true is 1 in 10^{168}. This is a larger number than most of us can grasp (though you may want to try to write it sometime). To give you some perspective on just how big this number is, consider these statistics from the book *Science Speaks* by Peter Stoner:

- If the state of Texas were buried in silver dollars two feet deep, it would be covered by 10^{17} silver dollars.

- In the history of the world, only 10^{11} people have supposedly ever lived. (I don't know who counted this.)

- There are 10^{17} seconds in 1 billion years.

- Scientists tell us that there are 10^{66} atoms in the universe and 10^{80} particles in the universe.

- Looking at just forty-eight prophecies out of more than three hundred, there is only a 1 in 10^{168} chance of Jesus not being who He said He was or of the Bible being wrong.

In probability theory, the threshold for an occurrence being absurd---translate that as "impossible"---is only 10^{50}. No thinking person who understands these probabilities can deny the reality of our faith or the Bible based on intellect. Every person who has set out to disprove the Judeo-Christian Scriptures on an empirical basis has ended up proving the Bible's authenticity and has, in most cases, become a believer.

These facts are more certain than any others in the world. However, not everyone who has come to realize the reliability and reality of these documents has become a believer. These intelligent people who understand the statistical impossibility that Jesus was not who He claimed to be and who yet do not make a decision for Christ are not senseless; they generally just have other issues. They allow these issues to stop them from enjoying the many experiential benefits that God offers them through His Word and the dynamic relationship they could have with Him, not to mention longer-term benefits. These people, of course, deserve love and prayer, because this is not just a matter of the intellect. If it were, every intelligent inquirer would be a believer. Rather, it is very much a matter of the heart, the emotions, and the spirit.

The truth of this statement was brought home to me in one very poignant situation. In this case, someone very near and dear to me said, "But Dad, this could have been anybody." No, this could not have been just anybody. The chance these prophecies could have been fulfilled in one person is so remote as to be absurd. That is impossible. Only one person in human history fulfilled these prophecies and that person is Jesus Christ. To claim otherwise is not intelligent, it is not smart, it is not well-considered, and it is not honest. It may be emotionally satisfying, but in all other respects it is self-delusional.

Printed in the United States
By Bookmasters